BLUE

NATURE'S SKETCHBOOK

by Marjolein Bastin

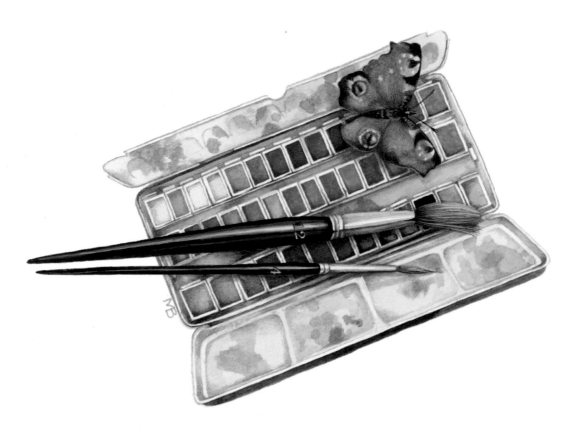

WRITTEN AND ILLUSTRATED BY
Marjolein Bastin

EDITED BY
Tara Pfeifer

STYLED BY
Charlie Mackaman / Mary Ann Odom

TECHNICAL SUPPORT
Kathy Smith-Williams

This book is for all of us who see in nature
a little part of ourselves...

Heartfelt thanks go out to my friends across the ocean—
Mary Ann, Charlie, Kathy and Tara, among many others—
whose help and support made Nature's Sketchbook possible.
It is wonderful and so inspiring to work with people
who share your same feelings...
And it is to them that I dedicate this book.

As I look through the pages again, I think to myself
that the best things in life are the people we love,
the places we've been, and the memories we've made
along the way.

My love of nature began when I was just a small child growing up near Utrecht in a picturesque town east of Amsterdam. We had a wonderful little house with a big garden overlooking the banks of the Vecht River. It was a quiet place surrounded by woodlands and moats and old, old houses. My very first memories are from the times my mother would take me out of my baby carriage and lay me in the middle of the soft green grass. I remember the grass stems growing so high above me, and I would look through them and see all kinds of beautiful flowers. I still recall so vividly the smell of the earth and the excitement of seeing everything new around me. I think I had the feeling before I could hardly walk or talk that each day was a gift with so many new things to discover.

As a little girl, I collected everything that excited me in nature. I would find earthworms and insects in our garden and sneak into the house with them and ask my mother for some bread. And she would tell me that I couldn't feed them because they had their own food in the grass and soil. Even back then, I felt I wanted to look after all of nature's creatures as if they were a part of my own family.

I also remember with great fondness my father showing me how to press the many beautiful flowers I discovered. He was a teacher and loved the hundreds of books that filled our home. He once handed me an old volume and told me to put my flowers in it, press down hard, put a stack of more books on top, and then wait. What a wonderful treat when I opened that book a few weeks later!

To this day, I'm grateful for all the encouragement my parents gave me. The first five or six years are so important in a child's life—I think you are given most everything for the rest of your life during those delicate years. Parents can hardly know or guess what's happening then, or what can happen, when they put their children in the garden or in the grass or in the park.

The first time I was old enough to hold a pencil was really the beginning of my drawing. As a little child, I already loved nature so much, I just had to do something with that feeling of excitement and wonder. I made my first serious paintings when I was around eight years old— paintings of pinecones and leaves and other simple things I found outdoors. I started with my palette and a piece of paper, and before too long a leaf would come to life like magic. And I thought to myself, "How amazing!" It was my way of holding forever the impression I loved so much in nature. When I was ten years old, I made a wonderful sketchbook with all sorts of natural drawings of little things which I thought of as my treasures. This was the beginning of my painting, and I haven't stopped since then.

I feel the main inspiration for everything I'm doing comes from nature itself. There were so many times in my life, especially during my younger years, when I sat completely alone in the woods, lost in contemplation and wonder. As I sat in silence, seeing everything, hearing even the slightest crackle, I realized we all are a _part_ of nature, part of something much larger than ourselves. I think the greatest feeling of completeness comes from this realization that we all have the same role in nature, even the tiniest creatures, and that all living things are related to each other. Those sights and smells and sounds are such a part of who I am today as a person and an artist. And what I felt then as a little girl, I still feel now. With my artwork, I try to show that this is our world. And because of that, we must be responsible, for when we ruin our nature, we ruin ourselves.

The pages that follow are glimpses into the nature journals I've kept through the seasons of so many years. I want to share my illustrations and personal reflections with the hope that they will touch you as much as nature has touched me.

When we open our eyes to nature, we see that things around us are never the same, and we discover— each hour, each day, each year— new things we didn't know and new creations that have their own stories to tell. There's just so much... more than enough for a lifetime of discovery!

Marjolein Bastin

Gardening is nice, very soothing to one's soul,
taking nature a bit into your hands, combining forms and colors...
I planted skimmia, with redbuds, and behind it the decorative reed mace.
And now just look! Everything is powdered sugar from the frost!

This is the time of year when I take such pleasure in daydreaming of the first signs of spring – when all of nature will wake from its winter sleep and come alive in a burst of color. It won't be much longer now...

SUNFLOWER
HELIANTHUS ANNUUS
GIANT GREYSTRIPE

Spring is just beginning on my worktable...

MB

GALANTHUS NIVALIS

Is it because the days are already getting longer
that the male blue tits are practicing their spring love songs?
I see them more and more often in the company of the females.
But it's still so cold!!

The time has come
for the first snowdrops
to begin blooming again.
I can hardly wait to see them!

It's a shame to pick too many...
Here I've gathered only a few snowdrops,
but it looks like much more with some
greenery added.

I was surprised by the bitten-off stems of the Christmas roses and assumed that the rabbits or the does were the culprits... until I saw a red-backed mouse carefully choose a flower, bite it off just behind the petals, and drag it with difficulty back to its home! I've seen the red-backed mice eat leaves and flowers before—they find bunches of anemones especially delicious—but I thought the Christmas roses were too big for them.

Then again, I also once saw a big blue violet come running past...

CROCUS

Could spring begin more vibrantly
or more frivolously than with crocuses
in all sorts of colors?
I grow the botanical varieties
which also appear in the woodland
that surrounds my house.

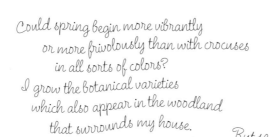

But these big ones grow near my window... and they so remind me
of my childhood,
when I would spend
countless hours
watching tiny bees
and bumblebees
creep into the flowers
to enjoy the nectar
and the pollen.

YELLOW

KING OF THE WHITES

PICKWICK

REMEMBRANCE

DUTCH YELLOW

MB

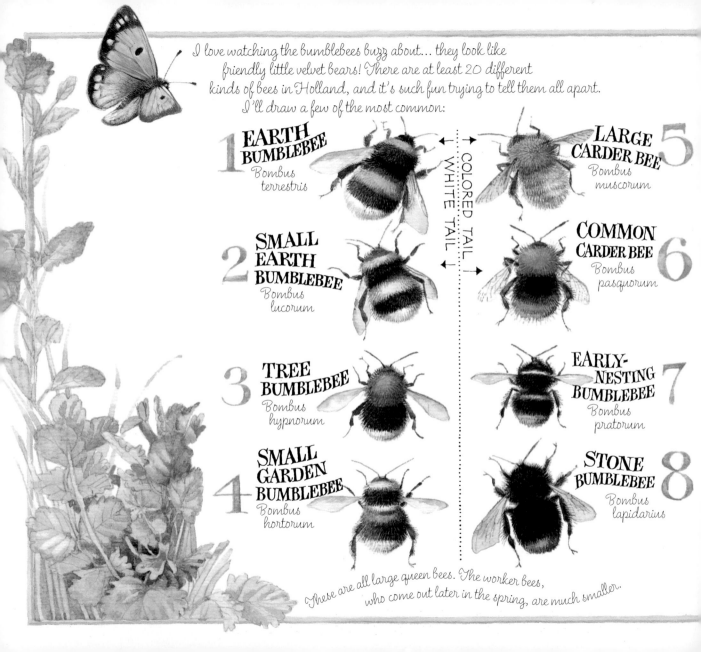

I love watching the bumblebees buzz about… they look like friendly little velvet bears! There are at least 20 different kinds of bees in Holland, and it's such fun trying to tell them all apart. I'll draw a few of the most common:

1 EARTH BUMBLEBEE
Bombus terrestris

2 SMALL EARTH BUMBLEBEE
Bombus lucorum

3 TREE BUMBLEBEE
Bombus hypnorum

4 SMALL GARDEN BUMBLEBEE
Bombus hortorum

← COLORED TAIL
WHITE TAIL →

LARGE CARDER BEE 5
Bombus muscorum

COMMON CARDER BEE 6
Bombus pasquorum

EARLY-NESTING BUMBLEBEE 7
Bombus pratorum

STONE BUMBLEBEE 8
Bombus lapidarius

These are all large queen bees. The worker bees, who come out later in the spring, are much smaller.

It can get very crowded in the wildflowers...

Red clover can only be pollinated by bumblebees.

I sat for quite some time today in a field of ground ivy. I so enjoyed watching the many different visitors these little blue flowers receive!

QUEEN

WORKER

This
beautiful
Butterfly has made
his life very difficult:
his tiny caterpillars
will not eat anything other
than these violets.
So for him and his kind,
there have to be these
beautiful blue violets.
And when they are not
there anymore,
the butterfly
will vanish, too.

NESTS AND NESTING BOXES

It's time for making a nest!
There's so terribly much building and brooding,
it is very difficult to keep track of it all.

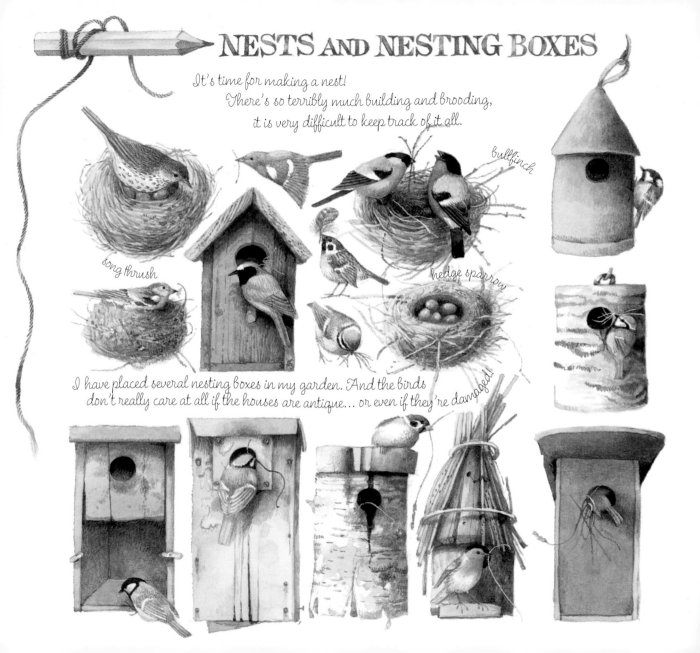

bullfinch

song thrush

hedge sparrow

I have placed several nesting boxes in my garden. And the birds
don't really care at all if the houses are antique... or even if they're damaged!

The whole day long, I just love to watch the birds from my worktable... They are so woven into my work!

Redbreasts nest everywhere— in woodpiles, sheds and bushes, but also among the vegetation on the ground. Stalks, plants and moss are worked into the nest, along with plant fluff and hair. Their offspring are fed a healthy diet of slugs, worms and insects.

Of course, you can always just nest in a tree... That's what the goldfinch does. He builds his nest of stalks, roots and webs and lines it with plant fluff or wool. Young goldfinches are first fed insects, but partially digested seeds are also on the menu.

The bullfinches like to nest in spruce trees. The female makes the nest with little twigs, roots and moss, and she lines it with hair and small blades of grass. Both father and mother take care of the young with insects and seeds.

And here we have a full page of nesting-box lovers...

The female nuthatch cushions the bottom of her nesting box with a thick layer of bark chips. At first she feeds her young tiny caterpillars, then later all kinds of insects which she picks out of branches and trunks.

Redstarts prefer to build in the hollows of trees — but a nesting-box will do just fine, too. The female builds the nest of plant blades, moss, hair and feathers. Together, mother and father feed their young a diet of insects, caterpillars, larvae and butterflies.

The tit is the most fond of nesting boxes... The bottom of her nest gets a thick moss mattress, and the inside is softly lined with animal hair or wool. The offspring are fed caterpillars.

This female finch built her nest in April.
Since then,
the young have
flown away,
so now I can take a closer look...

whiskers from a rabbit

thin blades of grass

feathers from a wood pigeon

hairs from Willem, the Labrador

feathers from a thrush

tuft of rabbit hair

And if it isn't a feather from its enemy, the wood owl!

one hair from a wild boar

Brown hairs from the mane of Skotta, my Iceland pony

Polystyrene balls. What a trendy finch!

webs and cocoons

insulation material

lots of pieces of moss

many strips of birch bark

small twigs of evergreen

some spruce needles

Black hairs from the mane of Rán, Sanna's Iceland pony

'A nest like this is another of nature's miracles!

This is the sweetest family portrait I've ever seen!

What a good idea it was to hang the owl house so that I can watch it from my worktable.

The little white owlet is a good sign that everything is going according to plan in the owl house!

On February third, for the first time, I saw the mother wood owl fly out of the birdhouse. After that, nothing happened for many days and I began to wonder. But one month later, I had hope again when I saw the owl change positions, sticking her wing tips out the hole each time she moved. She was bustling about so much that the birdhouse was shaking! When I counted backwards, I realized that she would have just started to sit on her eggs in February.

Owls begin to brood immediately after the first egg is laid, and every other day another egg is laid until there are three or four in the nest. The young also hatch a few days apart, giving the oldest a good head start on the youngest. The owl broods for about a month, so I figure this sweet little tyke is barely two weeks old. Do you suppose he's standing on his little sister's head to be able to reach the hole?

NB But I'm so easily distracted... Every other minute I look to see whether that crazy little head is peeping out over the edge of his hole!

Good morning, owl!

And flying exercises

I can do it this way, too.

In quick succession, two young wood owls fly out of the nest. They learn by doing, and these two have become quite a bit more skillful! Now there's yet a third baby owl in the birdhouse, but this shy one doesn't dare try to jump out and fly. Instead, he's been amusing himself for days with all sorts of climbing and flying exercises in the safety of his house. At night I hear his parents bringing him food.

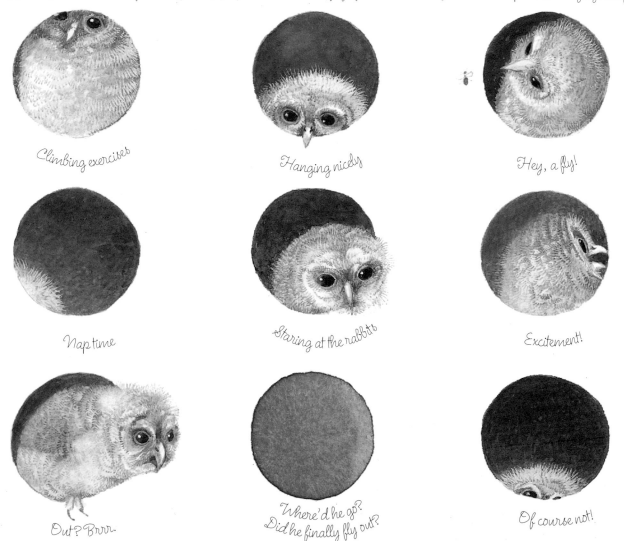

Climbing exercises

Hanging nicely

Hey, a fly!

Nap time

Staring at the rabbits

Excitement!

Out? Brrr.

Where'd he go?
Did he finally fly out?

Of course not!

One morning I discover the fledgling wood owl
on the big oak next to the house.
So finally he dared to jump out—into the big world.
What a sweet little guy!

The apple blossoms are now beginning to come out.
The high point of spring is seeing the tender, blushing blossoms
on those gnarled branches.

It mustn't freeze now...

How I envy you, dear little owl. The whole new world around you to discover... Wherever you may go, my best wishes are always with you.

MB

From morning until night, the rabbits play in the garden, delightfully running and jumping about! But WHY, oh why, must the dear bunnies eat all the radishes, the violets, the strawberries, and even the beautiful roses...?

RADISH

Isn't this a nice idea?

Radishes can be useful

POTENTILLA

The shrubby cinquefoil, potentilla fruticosa, is something that's nice to try in a large pot. It endlessly produces sweet little flowers, in every shade of white, yellow and orange, from June until late autumn.

This Adonis is for me!

ADONIS VERNALIS

Adonis

Water is a matter of life and death for the residents of pots. Especially when they're in the warm sun, they can dry out so quickly!

I keep my pots VERY close to the water faucet. That way I don't have to walk too far!

YELLOW

The Adonis and the Trollius make me beam with happiness because they remind me so much of Switzerland. There they grow wild.

For the bees, bumblebees and butterflies, there's Inula.

They grow just like this in the alpine meadow, among the cows.

TROLLIUS EUROPAEUS

Hey, shall we go to Switzerland again this summer?

MB

This beautiful bouquet
inspires me to paint with
such enthusiasm that there
is hardly enough room left for my words!

Just imagine this
in a jam jar on the table...
how opulent!

Bluebells here are protected, so you're not allowed to pick them.
That's why drawing is so nice— I can always sit among
the bluebells with my brushes and enjoy
their natural beauty.

MB

The cherry tree we planted
last year has just one cherry…

And I'm going to eat it NOW!

No time to sit and relax…

I must get back
to my work.

But the garden bench is not without its share of company.

The spiders and beetles loved
my old basket... it was perfect
for playing hide-and-seek.
To them, "old is beautiful,"
but I must admit that
as a flower basket,
it had become pretty rickety.

But here is my new one...
and I'll try this time not to leave it
out in the rain!

MB

STRAWBERRY

Can you also put strawberries in a flower basket?

PLUM

The plum family are preparing for a fruitful
year... They all produce a tasty fruit
with a large pit in the middle and
are most delicious when they are
ripened to perfection!

PRUNUS DOMESTICA

MB

MALUS COMMUNIS

Each year the apples begin to blossom near the close of April, and by mid-summer they are growing quite well.

In September we can harvest! Many varieties of apples grow in our little orchard....Golden Renetts, James Grieve, Cox's Orange, Granny Smith, Jonagold, and of course everybody's favorite, the old-fashioned red star apple!

Then we eat applesauce every day in all kinds of flavors!

APPLE

PRUNUS AVIUM

We have one old
and four young
cherry trees, which
bloom prosperously
by the end of April.

But amazingly,
we never get more than
this pudding bowl
full of cherries...
The blackbirds beat us to them...
and the starlings and jays
and squirrels and the crows. Ah, well.
It's nice to see that someone is
enjoying them!

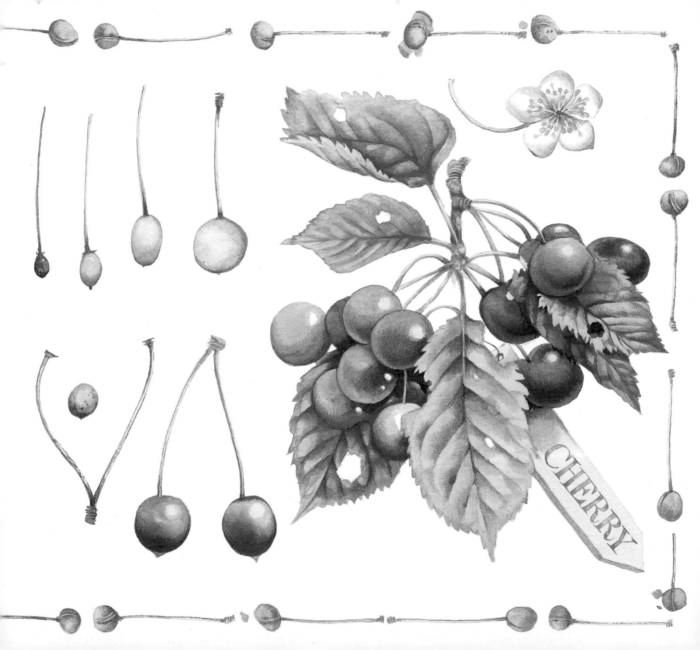

CHERRY

Our little herb garden is my most favorite place of all...

It is so quiet and smells delightful. Before I start cooking, I always go there to gather the perfect ingredients... and also when I just want to get away from everything. It is my refuge. Little Saar sits next to me on the bench. Unlike me, she considers the herb garden rather dull... but then again, we don't allow her off the paths, and she sticks strictly to the rules. But oh, poor thing... what exciting rustling behind the hedges! Mice, perhaps? Mmm. Frustrated, she again hops up next to me, looking at me with a slight tilt of her head...

The many varieties of Thyme complement many different foods.

Garden Lovage is called Magi herb. It is best in soups and sauces.

Marjoram attracts the butterflies and bees. I season almost everything with Marjoram.

Hyssop is a favorite of the bees.

Grey Sage adds flavor to meat dishes.

Lavender is the only herb that is meant for decorating but not for cooking.

It is such a temptation… one I can't resist…when there are
so many beautiful flowers around me, I have to pick some
and put them on my worktable in front of me so that
I may enjoy the beautiful colors. It's like bringing summer inside!

POPPY

SHIRLEY DOUBLE PAPAVER RHOEAS

Poppies are my favorite flower. I love
the way the poppy blooms— only for one day—
so colorfully and so expressively.
Imagine being able to say everything you want
in just one day and afterwards to spread
your thoughts in thousands of seeds
in all directions...

RED

...so that next year those thoughts appear everywhere!

PAPAVER ARGEMONE

PAPAVER RHOEAS

Blue in nature? Just take a look around...

Unforgettable is
the blue of the
chicory flowers
that bloom along
the river dikes.

BLUE

Or what about the faded hue of seashells from the deep blue sea...

MB

And how could I forget the bluethroat? He was my first sight of blue occurring in nature... and the bluest!

Quite some time ago I filled a flower box with blue violets...
The next year, I noticed more violets blooming near the box.
It's true they've become somewhat smaller, but their children and grandchildren are springing up everywhere!

The jay also drops a spot of blue.

Does there exist a more heavenly blue?

The forget-me-nots decorate the waterside like thousands of little blue stars.

NB. BLAUW   AZURRO   BLUE   BLEU   BLAU

VACATION!

Unanimously we choose Switzerland!
And while I'm packing my
paintbrushes, it all comes back again...
how, as a child, I put my
sketchbooks and tubes of paint
in my backpack... and how
I painted all the flowers
decorating the mountain
meadows and
huge boulders.
Even then, nature
held such
a fascination
for me.

ENZIAN
Beatenberg 1956

EDELWEISS

St. Moritz - Piz Nair 1961

Mürremen 1959

ALPEN-ASTER

ALPENROSE
Riffelberg 2222 m.

Zermatt 1963

That fondness for Switzerland runs like a thread
through our family. In 1927, when my father
was just sixteen years old, he and two friends
rode their bicycles there.
They slept in haystacks.

Many years ago, I sent
alpine rose cards like these
to my girlfriends with sayings
like "Greetings
from Switzerland! The weather is fine here!"

Gaston and I walk and climb a lot, trying hard
to keep up with the children...

BLUE

YELLOW

What a blessing that my painting
affords me a bit of rest as I pause
to give form and color to the wildflowers
in this beautiful landscape!

I feel like a child again here...
Some memories will never fade.
Words cannot begin to describe
how much I'm enjoying myself.

Another summer vacation, this time my first experience in a completely foreign landscape...
How exciting! I'll never forget the moment I spotted an American Goldfinch landing
on a long grass stem. Slowly... slowly, they bent over together. This is my next drawing,
I thought then.

At home
in Holland,
I can name
nearly everything
that flies, crawls,
grows and blooms.
But here in the midst
of a huge prairie
in the Midwest,
there's so much
I don't recognize.
Total amazement!
And I know
this feeling well...
It reminds me of when
I was that small child
in the garden so long ag

I recognize a few of the flowers around me, for in Holland we grow them in our gardens. I didn't know that here they grow wild in the prairie. And that bird over there... What do you call him?

We also have dragonflies, but they look a bit different than this one.

And who is this little green grasshopper?

This is so exciting!

Saar loves to keep me company in the greenhouse. She wants to make herself useful, looking at me as if to say, "Okay, you clean out the old seed boxes and I'll clear out the mice for you."

As usual, all her efforts are fortunately in vain.

A lot of flowerpots fall over, though...

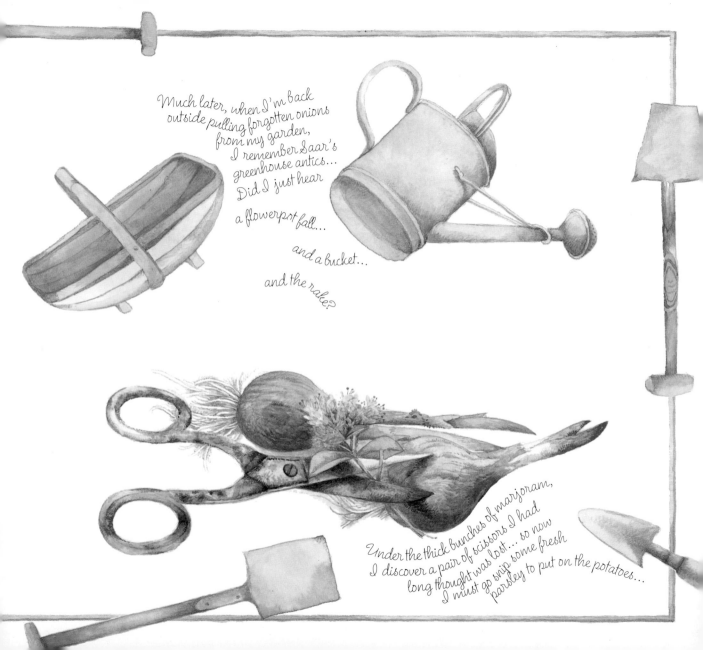

Much later, when I'm back
outside pulling forgotten onions
from my garden,
I remember Saar's
greenhouse antics...
Did I just hear

a flowerpot fall...

and a bucket...

and the rake?

Under the thick bunches of marjoram,
I discover a pair of scissors I had
long thought was lost... so now
I must go snip some fresh
parsley to put on the potatoes...

Who says that autumn is somber? Could it be any more colorful?

English Oak

Birch

It seems as though nature has saved all its splendor and beauty until this moment.
What an emotional good-bye. And isn't it true that only when you leave,
you say the things you've wanted to say all along?

Hawthorn

Blueberry

Blackberry

American Oak

Juneberry

I dry the most beautiful leaves in my telephone book…

Maple

Elder

Willow

Back in America, in late autumn... Again, the landscape is totally different,
but this time the weather is cold, the sky grey.

After a nice ginger cookie party in a wonderful farmhouse near Kearney, Missouri, we decide upon
a long nature walk. The woods are brown and greyed from the rain, but far from dull!

Ah, and then I saw it... my very first cardinal... perched on a white tree trunk. My heart was pounding
with excitement and emotion! This is beautiful,
I thought. I have to show this to everyone...
I want to share this beauty. And so
I made the drawing on the following pages,
forever known as the "Kearney Cardinal."

American robins around the house,
perching on nice old fences...

I brought home such a beautiful bouquet of fall treasures. Most of the berries and fruits, I don't even know!

We were soaking wet, but inside it was pretty and warm and the tea was ready. We toweled ourselves dry and enjoyed again the fresh-baked cookies.

ILEX
AQUIFOLIUM

PICEA SITCHENSIS

Winter is a time to stand still,
to contemplate and to wonder.
For a short while, the busy
world slows down a bit...

PINUS NIGRA

PICEA ABIES

ANEMONE CORONARIA

Winter is also the time when we bring nature into
our homes together with fond memories of our
family and friends.

My parents are not with us anymore. I miss them very much.
But when I'm in the woods around our house picking holly branches and
pinecones for our holiday table, I feel my mother there with me.
And my father, too. Somewhere in me. All the ones we love will live
forever in our hearts.

This seems to be the end of my book, but how can it be, because nature's story never ends. Nature is always full of new promises... Do you see the buds on the trees, the leaves and flowers still carefully hidden? Did you hear the first songthrush early this morning?
And when you kneel down, perhaps you will discover the first snowdrop. Soon it will be spring again, and everything—all of life—will start over.
You only have to open your eyes to see it, to enjoy it and to feel it— such incredible riches all around us, every day.

Marjolein Bastin